FA
R
with
BEER & CIDER

Illustrated with scenes of country life

SALMON

Index

Apple, Raisin and Cider Teabread 42
Beef in Stout 3
Beery Beef with Crusty Topping 5
Boiled Bacon and Cider Sauce 21
Buttered Apples 47
Carbonnade of Beef 7
Cider-Baked Fish 31
Cider Baked Pears 43
Dartmouth Pie 22
Farmer's Brew 13
Goulash 8
Grayling in Beer 35
Ham Baked with Cider and Thyme 18
Hereford Cider Cake 40
Honeyed Welsh Lamb 15
Mackerel in Cider and Apple Sauce 37
Midsummer Pudding and Cider Sauce 38
Painswick Gammon in Cider 19
Quick Beef in Beer 11
Rabbit Stew 27
Ragged Rabbit with Cider 29
Roast Veal with Beer 14
Salmon in Cider 32
Shearers Stew 16
Spiced Beef 6
Spicy Stewed Pears 46
Stuffed Pork Chops baked in Cider 23
Stuffed Pork in Cider Sauce 26
Somerset Fish Casserole 30
Trout with Herbs and Cider 34
Upcott Pork 24
Wassail Bowl 45
Welsh Beef Stew 10
Yorkshire Parkin 39

Cover pictures *front:* "A Refreshing Glass" *by William Shayer*
back: "The Farm Cart" *by Myles Birket Foster*
Title page: "The Country Inn" *by Myles Birket Foster*

Printed and published by Dorrigo, Manchester, England

Beef in Stout

A stew that dates from the 19th century, when it was often made with porter, a dark brown ale which, like stout, produces a fine, dark gravy.

2 lb. stewing steak, cubed
1 tablespoon oil
A walnut of butter
2 onions, sliced
2 tablespoons flour
Salt and black pepper
2 carrots, sliced
½ pint stout
1 teaspoon soft brown sugar
Chopped fresh parsley for garnish

Heat the oil and butter in a large saucepan and cook the meat until lightly browned. Remove and set aside. Add the onions and fry until softened. Stir in the flour and seasoning, then return the meat to the saucepan with the carrots, stout and sugar. Stir well and bring to the boil, then cover and simmer gently for 2 to 2½ hours or until the meat is tender. Serve garnished with chopped parsley and accompanied by mashed potatoes and a green vegetable. Serves 4 to 6.

If desired, a half-and-half mix of Guinness and water can be used for the gravy and a few sliced mushrooms added to the stew. Alternatively, this dish can be cooked in the oven at 350°F or Mark 4 for the same length of time.

"At the Bell Inn" by William Shayer

Beery Beef with Crusty Topping

A delicious, rich stew with a tasty bread topping.

1½ lbs. lean braising beef   2 slices back bacon, chopped   2 tablespoons oil
1 oz. butter   2 tablespoons flour   ½ pint bitter beer   ½ pint beef stock
1 teaspoon caster sugar   2 cloves garlic, peeled and crushed
2 medium onions, skinned and thinly sliced   2 carrots, peeled and sliced
1 bouquet garni   Salt and freshly ground black pepper

TOPPING

6 thick slices of white bread, buttered and spread with 1-2 tablespoons of grainy mustard
3 oz. Cheddar cheese, grated

Set oven to 325°F or Mark 3. Heat the oil and butter together in a frying pan, cut the meat into 1 inch cubes and fry a little at a time until well browned; place in a large casserole dish. Fry the bacon and transfer to the dish. Add the flour to the fat and cook, stirring until lightly browned. Gradually add the beer and stock and stir until the sauce thickens. Add one teaspoon of sugar. Put the garlic, onions and carrots in the casserole dish with the meat and pour the sauce over. Put in the bouquet garni and season with salt and pepper. Cook for 2½ hours until the meat is tender. The casserole will benefit by being stirred halfway through cooking. Remove the bouquet garni and arrange the bread on top of the meat. Sprinkle the cheese over and grill until the cheese bubbles. Serves 4-6.

Spiced Beef

Eaten hot or cold, Spiced Beef is traditionally served on Christmas Day or Boxing Day, decorated with holly.

4 lb. rolled salted silverside
1 onion, sliced
1 small turnip, sliced
3 carrots, sliced
1 bayleaf
Water, stout or brown ale
12 cloves
2 oz. soft brown sugar
Juice of 1 lemon
½ teaspoon each ground cinnamon, allspice and nutmeg
1 level teaspoon mustard powder

Soak the meat in cold water overnight. Next day, rinse well and tie up with kitchen string to form a firm, neat joint. Put the onion, turnip and carrots in a large saucepan, place the meat on top, add the bayleaf then cover with cold water or a mixture of water and stout or brown ale. Bring to the boil, skim, then cover and simmer gently for 3½ to 4 hours. Leave to cool completely in the liquid. Set oven to 350°F or Mark 4. Drain the meat very well, place in a roasting tin and stick with the cloves. Mix together all the remaining ingredients and spread over the meat. Bake for 40 minutes, basting from time to time. Remove the string and serve hot or cold. Serves 4 to 6.

Carbonnade of Beef

Brown ale and long, slow cooking combine to make this classic, full-flavoured stew.

1½ lb. stewing steak, trimmed and cut into 1½ inch cubes
2 large onions, sliced 1 garlic clove, crushed
1 tablespoon plain flour 8 fl.oz. beef stock
13 fl.oz. brown ale Salt and pepper
1 bouquet garni Pinch of grated nutmeg
Pinch of soft light brown sugar
1 teaspoon red wine vinegar

Set the oven at 325°F or Mark 3. Melt the butter or margarine in a heavy-bottomed frying pan, add the beef and fry quickly until browned. Transfer the beef to a casserole and keep hot. Add the onions to the fat remaining in the pan and fry until lightly browned, then stir in the garlic and fry over gentle heat for 1 minute. Pour off any excess fat from the pan to leave about 1 tablespoon. Add the flour to the onions and garlic and cook, stirring constantly, until lightly browned. Gradually stir in the stock and ale. Add salt and pepper to taste. Add the bouquet garni, nutmeg, brown sugar and vinegar. Bring to the boil, then pour the liquid over the beef in the casserole. Cover and bake for 1½-2 hours or until the beef is tender. Remove the bouquet garni. Serve immediately, straight from the casserole. Serves 6.

Goulash

Believed to originate from Hungary, goulash is delicious, tasty and warming.

1½ lb. stewing steak, cut into ½ inch cubes
2 level tablespoons seasoned flour
2 medium sized onions, skinned and chopped
1 green pepper, seeded and chopped
2 tablespoons fat or oil 2 level teaspoons paprika
3 level tablespoons tomato paste Little grated nutmeg
Salt and pepper 2 oz. flour ¼ pint stock
8 oz. can tomatoes ¼ pint beer
Bouquet garni 5 fl.oz. carton soured cream

Coat the meat with seasoned flour. Fry the onions and pepper lightly in the fat or oil for about 3-4 minutes. Add the meat and fry lightly on all sides until golden brown – about 5 minutes. Add the paprika and fry for about a minute longer. Stir in the tomato paste, nutmeg, seasoning and flour and cook for a further 2-3 minutes. Add the stock, tomatoes, beer and bouquet garni, put into a casserole and cook in the oven at 325°F or Mark 3 for 1½-2 hours. Remove the bouquet garni and spoon over the soured cream. Serve with sauerkraut or with a green salad.

"Among the Corn Stooks" by Edmund Warren

Welsh Beef Stew

This all-in-one stew would sometimes be used to provide two meals; meat and vegetables for one and broth for another.

1 oz. butter
1½ lb. stewing steak, cubed
8 oz. streaky bacon rashers, de-rinded and cut into four
1 tablespoon flour
1½ to 2 pints water
2 onions, peeled and sliced
2 carrots, peeled and sliced
2 small turnips, peeled and cubed
1 heaped dessertspoon fresh chopped herbs (parsley, thyme, sage, etc. mixed)
Salt and white pepper
¼ pint cider
½ lb. potatoes, weighed after peeling
3 leeks, washed and trimmed
Chopped fresh parsley for garnish

Melt the butter in a large saucepan and fry the beef and bacon lightly, then sprinkle over the flour and fry for a further minute. Add the water and bring to the boil, then cover and simmer for 40 minutes. Allow to cool slightly and skim, then add the onions, carrots and turnips, herbs and seasoning and bring to the boil. Add the cider, cover and simmer for 1 hour. Add the potatoes and leeks, cover and simmer for a further 20 to 30 minutes. Serve, sprinkling each portion with a little finely chopped parsley. Serves 4 to 6.

Quick Beef in Beer

If you are in a hurry this is an excellent, filling recipe.

1½ lb. cooked lean beef, minced   1 onion, grated
1 garlic clove, crushed   7 fl.oz. beer
Salt and pepper

Put all the ingredients in a dish and leave for 30 minutes. Transfer to a saucepan and simmer for 15 to 20 minutes, or until completely heated through. Season to taste with salt and pepper. Can be eaten with vegetables or rice. Serves 4.

"A peasant family outside a woodland cottage" by William Shayer

Farmer's Brew

A delicious stew which is cooked in beer.

1½ lb. stewing steak
1 oz. seasoned flour
2 oz. butter
4 oz. onions, sliced
1 oz. granulated sugar
Pinch of mustard powder
Sprig of fresh thyme
1 bayleaf
Salt and pepper
10 fl.oz. Scottish ale
5 fl.oz. beef stock

Set oven to 400°F or Mark 6. Slice the meat into thin strips and toss in the seasoned flour. Melt the butter in a heavy ovenproof casserole dish and brown the meat and onions. Add the sugar, mustard, thyme and bayleaf and season well. Bring up to heat, cover and cook in the oven for 10 minutes. Remove from the oven, add the beer and stock and bring to the boil. Reduce the oven temperature to 325°F or Mark 3. Return the casserole to the oven and cook for a further 1½ hours. Serve on a bed of mashed potato. Serves 4 to 6.

Roast Veal with Beer

This veal dish is roasted with carrots and onions.

3 lb. loin of veal
2 oz. dripping or lard
Salt and pepper
2-3 carrots, pared and sliced
2-3 onions, skinned and sliced
½ pint beer
1 bayleaf
2 cloves
1 tablespoon flour

Spread the meat thickly with the dripping or lard and put it in a meat tin. Season with salt and pepper. Add the carrots and onions, and roast in the oven at 425°F or Mark 7 for 30 minutes. Pour the beer over the meat, add the bayleaf and cloves and return it to the oven. Turn down the heat to 375°F or Mark 5 and cook the meat until tender, basting frequently – allow 30 minutes per 1 lb. When the meat is cooked place it on a serving dish. Blend the flour with the juices in the tin, heat until boiling, then strain over the meat.

Honeyed Welsh Lamb

A leg of Welsh lamb coated with honey and roasted,
served with cider and honey gravy.

4 lb. leg of lamb
6 tablespoons Welsh clover honey
Sprig of rosemary
Salt and freshly ground pepper
½ pint cider

Set oven to 400°F or Mark 6. Place the leg of lamb on kitchen foil in a roasting tin. Brush with 4 tablespoons of warm honey and season with salt and pepper. Place the sprig of rosemary on top of the joint. Draw up the foil to form a tent and roast for 15 minutes. Lower the heat to 350°F or Mark 4 and continue roasting for 1½ hours until the juice just runs pink or longer if preferred well done. Open up the foil to crisp and brown the skin for the last 20 minutes of cooking time. Remove the lamb from the oven and keep warm. Pour off the fat from the pan and make the gravy from the meat residue, adding half a pint of cider and 2 tablespoons of honey. Reduce to two thirds volume by boiling. Serve with roast potatoes and green vegetables. Serves 6.

Shearers Stew

A simple stew made with leg of lamb and brown ale.

1½ lb. leg of lamb, trimmed and cut into 1 inch cubes
3 tablespoons cooking oil
1 oz. butter
2 onions, thinly sliced
1 oz. flour
½ pint brown ale
½ pint lamb stock
2 carrots, sliced
Salt and pepper
4 thick slices of fresh white bread, cut into triangles

Set oven to 350°F or Mark 4. Heat the oil in a frying pan, add the butter and, when hot, brown the lamb in small batches and transfer to a casserole dish. Add the onions to the frying pan and cook gently until soft. Stir in the flour and cook for 2 to 3 minutes. Remove from the heat and stir in the brown ale and stock. Return to the heat and bring to the boil, stirring. Add the carrots and seasoning to the casserole. Pour the liquid over all, cover and cook for 1 hour. Remove from the oven and stir well. Dip the bread into the liquid and arrange attractively on top. Return to the oven, uncovered, and cook for a further 30 minutes. Serves 4 to 6.

“Resting” by William Millner

Ham baked with Cider and Thyme

The farmer's wife and her helpers would bake an enormous ham for the harvest table.

3-4 lb. boned and rolled gammon joint
2 onions, peeled and quartered
1 leek, sliced
1 stick celery, sliced
10 cloves
Parsley stalks
2 bay leaves
1 tablespoon chopped fresh thyme
4 oz. demerara sugar
4 oz. Dijon mustard
½ pint dry cider

Soak the gammon in cold water for 12 to 24 hours if necessary, depending on how salty it seems. Place in a large pan, cover with cold water and bring to the boil. Skim off any scum. Add the onions, leek, celery, cloves, parsley, bay leaves and thyme. Cover and simmer slowly for 1½ hours. Set oven to 425°F or Mark 7. When cooked, place the gammon in a roasting tin and remove the skin, leaving the fat intact. Score the fat into diamond shapes. Mix the sugar with sufficient mustard to make a paste. Brush over the scored fat and bake for 35 to 40 minutes. Mix the remaining mustard and cider and baste the ham occasionally after the first 5 minutes. When the fat is golden, transfer to a warm plate and leave to rest for at least 10 minutes before carving. Serve hot or cold.

Painswick Gammon in Cider

If preferred, bacon chops can be used in place of the gammon rashers.

4 gammon rashers, rinds removed and the fat nicked to prevent curling
1 level tablespoon made English mustard
1 oz. demerara sugar ½ pint dry, still cider
½ oz. butter 1½ oz. flour
Salt and black pepper (optional)
Parsley sprigs to garnish

Set oven to 400°F or Mark 6. Mix together the mustard and sugar with enough cider to make a smooth paste. Spread over the rashers and leave for 30 minutes. Place the rashers in a large ovenproof dish and cook for 15 minutes. Melt the butter in a saucepan and stir in the flour together with the seasoning if desired. Add the remaining cider and cook, stirring continuously, until the sauce has boiled and is smooth and thick. Pour over the rashers, and cook for a further 15 minutes. Serve garnished with parsley sprigs. Serves 4.

"Travellers Resting at a Country Inn" by William Shayer

Boiled Bacon and Cider Sauce

A traditional Herefordshire recipe.

2 to 3 lb. bacon joint   Water
1 carrot, peeled and chopped into chunks
1 onion, peeled and quartered   1 bayleaf   6 peppercorns

Cider Sauce:
½ pint dry cider   2 bayleaves   2 sprigs parsley   4 cloves
Pinch of dry mustard   Salt and black pepper
½ pint thick, well-flavoured brown gravy

Place the bacon joint in a saucepan, cover with water and bring to the boil. Discard the water, add the remaining ingredients to the bacon joint and add sufficient fresh water to cover. Bring to the boil, then simmer gently, allowing 20 minutes to the lb. plus 20 minutes over. Drain the bacon well. Remove the rind and serve hot with boiled potatoes, carrots and celery and accompanied by the Cider Sauce.
CIDER SAUCE: Place the cider, herbs, spices and seasoning in a saucepan, bring to the boil and simmer until reduced approximately by half. Stir in the gravy, bring to the boil and simmer, stirring from time to time, until reduced approximately by one third. Strain into a sauceboat and serve with the boiled bacon. Serves 4 to 6.

Dartmouth Pie

A Devonshire favourite, delicious when served with warm clotted cream.

1½ lb. of leg of pork, cut into thin slices
3 medium onions, peeled and sliced
3 large cooking apples, peeled, cored and sliced
2 tablespoons brown sugar mixed with a pinch of ground nutmeg and a pinch of ground cinnamon
½ pint dry cider 8 oz. shortcrust pastry

Set oven to 400°F or Mark 6. Place a layer of thinly sliced pork in a deep oven-proof dish. Cover this with a layer of apples and then half of the sugar-and-spice mixture. On top of the sugar place a layer of onions. Repeat these three layers and then pour the cider over all. Roll out the pastry on a floured surface and use to cover the dish, making two holes for the steam to escape; or use a pie funnel. Bake for 20 minutes. Reduce the oven temperature to 300°F or Mark 2. Cover the pastry with foil to prevent burning and continue the cooking for a further 60 minutes. Serve hot with warm clotted cream.

Stuffed Pork Chops baked in Cider

A traditional West Country dish.

4 x 8 oz. pork chops ½-¾ pint dry cider
1 oz. butter for browning the chops

Stuffing
1 oz. butter 1 medium onion, peeled and chopped
1 medium cooking apple, peeled, cored and grated
6 prunes, stoned and chopped 1 oz. walnuts, finely chopped
1 small egg, beaten 4 tablespoons fresh white breadcrumbs
Salt and pepper

Set oven to 425°F or Mark 7. For the stuffing, melt 1 oz. of butter and cook the onion gently until soft. Remove from the heat and add all the remaining stuffing ingredients. Slit the outside edges of the chops to make pockets and push the stuffing into them. Melt the remaining 1 oz. butter in a frying pan and quickly brown each chop. Transfer to an ovenproof dish and pour over about ½ pint of cider; enough to cover the bottom of the dish. Bake for approximately 30-40 minutes until the meat is tender. During cooking, baste the chops from time to time and add more cider if needed. The chops should be served hot with the reduced, syrupy cider liquid poured over them.

Upcott Pork

The apple, cheese, cream and pork complement each other perfectly in this tasty Devonshire recipe.

2 oz. butter 2 lb. pork tenderlion, sliced thinly
6 oz. Curworthy cheese (or Cheddar), grated
1 small onion, peeled and finely diced
2 medium eating apples, peeled and sliced
½ pint dry cider ¼ pint double cream
Salt and pepper

Melt the butter in a frying pan and sauté the thin slices of pork for 5 or 6 minutes until cooked through. Place on a hot dish and interleave with layers of grated cheese; set aside and keep warm. Sauté the onions in the same pan, add the apples and cook until soft. Add the cider and, when bubbling, stir in the cream. Cook for 3 or 4 minutes. Season. Pour the sauce over the pork and cheese, and serve.

“At the Cricket Match” by John Reid

Stuffed Pork in Cider Sauce

A Herefordshire farmhouse recipe.

1 to 1½ lb. pork tenderloin, cut in half lengthwise
2 oz. butter 1 large onion, peeled and chopped
2 rashers streaky bacon, de-rinded and chopped
1 large apple, peeled, cored and chopped
2 oz. breadcrumbs 1 tablespoon fresh chopped parsley
1 teaspoon fresh chopped sage Salt and black pepper
1 egg, beaten 1 tablespoon flour ½ pint dry cider

Flatten the two pieces of tenderloin slightly. Melt the butter and fry the onion until soft, then add the bacon and apple and fry for 1 to 2 minutes. Stir into the breadcrumbs in a bowl, add the herbs and seasoning and bind with the beaten egg. Spread the filling over one half of the tenderloin, top with the other half and tie in three or four places with kitchen string to keep its shape during roasting. Set oven to 350°F or Mark 4. Place in a roasting tin with a little oil and roast for 1 hour, basting occasionally. Remove from the tin, cut off the string, place on a heated serving dish and keep warm. Stir the flour into the juices in the tin, add the cider and bring to the boil, stirring. Serve the tenderloin with the sauce poured over, accompanied by creamed potatoes, mushrooms and grilled tomatoes. Serves 4.

Rabbit Stew

The ale and ketchup give a rich flavour to this tasty game recipe.

1 rabbit, jointed	**½ pint ale or stout**
Seasoned flour	**½ teacup mushroom ketchup**
1 oz. butter	**Nutmeg**
½ pint good stock	**Lemon peel**

1 onion stuck with 1 or 2 cloves

Set oven to 350 °F or Mark 4. Wash and dry the joints. Roll them in the flour and fry in the butter until brown. Add the stock, ale, ketchup, lemon peel and onion. Grate some nutmeg over all. Cook 1–2 hours, according to the age of the rabbit. Alternatively this could be simmered on top of the stove for a similar time.

“An Old Roadside Inn” by William Shayer

Ragged Rabbit with Cider

At one time rabbit formed a very important part of any country diet.

1 lb. boneless rabbit cut into 1 inch pieces
2 tablespoons flour seasoned with salt and pepper
2 tablespoons sunflower oil   1 oz. butter
2 medium onions, peeled and diced
4 oz. streaky bacon, chopped
¼ pint chicken or rabbit stock
¼ pint dry cider   1 tablespoon tomato pureé
2-3 sprigs fresh thyme   4 oz. button mushrooms

Set oven to 325°F or Mark 3. Toss the rabbit pieces in the seasoned flour. Heat the oil in a frying pan and when hot add the butter. Brown the rabbit pieces a few at a time and transfer to a casserole dish. Add the onions and bacon to the pan and cook gently until the onions are soft. Stir in the remaining seasoned flour and cook for 2–3 minutes. Remove from the heat and add the stock, cider and tomato pureé. Return to the heat and stir until boiling. Pour over the rabbit and add the fresh thyme. Cover the casserole and cook for 1 hour; add the mushrooms and cook for a further 30 minutes or until the rabbit is tender. Serve hot with fresh vegetables.

Somerset Fish Casserole

A substantial lunch or supper dish of cod or haddock flavoured with cider.

2 lb. cod or haddock fillet
2½ oz. butter
Salt and pepper
4 oz. mushrooms, sliced
4 oz. tomatoes, skinned and sliced
½ pint cider
Butter for dotting
1 lb. creamed mashed potatoes
Grated cheese for sprinkling
Tomato slices and parsley sprigs to garnish

SAUCE

1½ oz. butter 1½ oz. flour Fish liquid

Set oven to 375° F or Mark 5. Butter an ovenproof casserole dish. Cut the fish into small cubes and arrange in the dish. Season. Add the mushrooms and tomatoes, pour over the cider and dot with butter. Cover and bake for 25 minutes. Carefully strain off the liquid. To make the sauce, melt the butter in a pan, stir in the flour and gradually stir in the fish liquid. Bring to the boil and cook for a few minutes, stirring, to thicken. Increase oven to 450°F or Mark 8. Pour the sauce over the fish in the dish. Arrange a border of mashed potato, sprinkle the fish with grated cheese and garnish with tomato slices. Return to the oven, uncovered, for the cheese to bubble and to brown. Serve garnished with parsley. Serves 4 to 6.

Cider-baked Fish

Cider and fish make a pleasant combination in this Worcestershire recipe.

4 cod or other white fish steaks
A little butter
4 sprigs parsley
Salt and black pepper
½ pint cider

1½ oz. butter
1½ oz. flour
Milk
1 tablespoon fresh, chopped parsley
Parsley sprigs, for garnish

Set oven to 350°F or Mark 4. Wipe the fish steaks, place in an ovenproof casserole and season lightly. Dot each steak with a little butter and place a parsley sprig on top. Pour over the cider, cover and bake for 20 minutes. Reserving the liquid, carefully remove the fish steaks, drain well, place on a heated serving dish and keep warm. Melt the butter in a saucepan and stir in the flour. Strain the fish liquid and make up to about ¾ pint with the milk. Add to the flour mixture, a little at a time, stirring continually until the sauce boils and thickens. Season, stir in the chopped parsley and pour into a warmed sauceboat. Serve the fish steaks, garnished with parsley sprigs, with creamed potatoes, green peas and grilled tomatoes and with the sauce served separately. Serves 4.

Salmon in Cider

The Salmon is baked with shallots and basted with cider.
The cider 'cuts' the rich oiliness of the salmon.

2-3 lb. middle cut salmon, cleaned and washed
1½ oz. butter Salt and black pepper
½ teaspoon ground nutmeg
2 small shallots, peeled and chopped
1 dessertspoon fresh chopped parsley
2½-3 fl.oz. dry cider

Set oven to 375°F or Mark 5. Cut the salmon into 4 equal slices and arrange in a well buttered ovenproof dish. Season with salt, pepper and nutmeg. Mix together the shallots and parsley and sprinkle over the salmon. Dot with butter, then pour on the cider. Bake for 15-20 minutes, basting frequently. Serve with buttered, boiled potatoes and with tomato sauce, to which a little of the strained cooking liquid has been added. Serves 4.

"A Refreshing Glass" by William Shayer

Trout with Herbs and Cider

Noted for its cider-making, cider is a popular ingredient in both savoury and sweet dishes in Herefordshire.

4 prepared trout   1 oz. seasoned flour   1½ to 2 oz. butter
2 tablespoons fresh, finely chopped mixed herbs – parsley, thyme, basil etc.
Juice of half a lemon   4 tablespoons dry cider
2 to 3 tablespoons single cream
Lemon slices and sprigs of herbs for garnish

Cut each trout into two fillets and coat in seasoned flour. Melt the butter in a frying pan and stir in the herbs. Add the trout fillets and fry for 3 to 5 minutes, turning once. Add the lemon juice and cider, cover and simmer over a very low heat for a further 3 to 5 minutes. Carefully remove the trout fillets, place on a heated serving dish and keep warm, then stir the cream into the cider mixture and heat through. Pour over the trout fillets and serve garnished with lemon slices and herb sprigs and accompanied by boiled potatoes. Serves 4.

Grayling in Beer

The grayling is a silvery fish, a relation of the salmon and trout, found in swift-flowing rivers. Its flesh is said to have the scent of thyme.

4 grayling, gutted, scaled and well washed
1 pint beer
2 level teaspoons grated horseradish
1 teaspoon grated lemon rind
Salt Black pepper
Sprigs of fresh thyme ¾ oz. butter
Lemon slices and thyme sprigs for garnish

Using a sharp knife, make three or four scores on each side of the fish. Place in a large, deep frying pan and pour on the beer. Sprinkle with the horseradish and lemon rind and season well. Top with thyme sprigs. Bring to the boil, cover and simmer until the fish is tender – about 15 minutes. Very carefully remove the fish from the cooking liquid, drain and place on a warm serving dish. Strain the cooking liquid and measure ¼-pint into a saucepan. Add the butter, heat through and pour the sauce over the fish. Serve garnished with lemon slices and thyme sprigs and accompanied by creamed horseradish sauce and brown bread and butter. Serves 4.

"The Six Bells" by Helen Allingham

Mackerel in Cider and Apple Sauce

Mackerel is best eaten very fresh. With its characteristic blue-black markings, a creamy coloured flesh and a distinctive flavour, it is in season from October to July.

1 oz. butter ½ onion, finely chopped 1 tablespoon cornflour
4 mackerel, filleted ¾ pint dry cider 1 bayleaf
Salt & pepper to season
2 small dessert apples, peeled, cored and sliced thinly

Melt the butter in a large non-stick frying pan, add the onion and cook until translucent. Add the cornflour and cook for 1 minute stirring continuously. Slowly add the cider whilst continuing to stir. Season to taste and add the mackerel fillets. Cover tightly, reduce the heat and allow to simmer gently for 15 minutes until the mackerel is tender. Remove mackerel and keep warm. Turn up the heat slightly, add the apple slices to the pan and simmer for 4-5 minutes until the sauce is thick and reduced. Pour the sauce over the fish and serve. Serves 4.

Midsummer Pudding and Cider Sauce

This steamed suet pudding is traditionally served with cider sauce.

8 oz. prepared suet pastry
1½ lb. prepared fruit, redcurrants, raspberries etc.
4 oz. sugar or to taste
1 scant dessertspoon water containing a squeeze of lemon juice

Cider Sauce:
1 pint cider ¼ lb. sugar 2 to 3 oz. butter

Roll out the pastry on a lightly floured surface and use three-quarters to line a buttered 1½ to 2 pint pudding basin. Add half the fruit, sprinkle over the sugar, then add the remaining fruit and spoon over the water with lemon juice. Roll out the remaining pastry to form a lid and place on the pudding, wetting and sealing the edges well. Cover with buttered greaseproof paper and seal with kitchen foil. Steam over a saucepan of boiling water for 1½ to 2 hours. Serve with Cider Sauce, custard or cream. Serves 4 to 6.

CIDER SAUCE: Simmer the cider and sugar together to form a light syrup, stirring from time to time. Cut the butter into small pieces and whisk into the mixture. Pour into a sauceboat and serve at once.

Yorkshire Parkin

This is a variation of parkin in which beer is incorporated with black treacle in the mixture.

½ lb. flour
1 teaspoon bicarbonate of soda
3 oz. butter, softened
3 oz. lard
4 oz. fine oatmeal
4 oz. medium oatmeal
2 teaspoons ground ginger
1 egg, beaten
1 lb. black treacle
½ pint beer

Set oven to 350° F or Mark 4. Grease and flour an 8 inch square shallow cake tin or equivalent. Sift the flour and bicarbonate of soda into a bowl and rub in the butter and lard until the mixture resembles breadcrumbs. Add all the oatmeal and the ground ginger and mix together with the beaten egg to a fairly stiff consistency. Put the treacle and beer into a pan and warm together over a gentle heat. Add gradually to the oatmeal mixture and mix well to a soft, dropping consistency. Spoon into the tin and bake for 45 to 60 minutes until golden. Leave in the tin to cool and then cut into squares.

Hereford Cider Cake

A cake traditionally served at Harvest Suppers.

4 oz. butter 4 oz. caster sugar 2 eggs
8 oz. flour Pinch of salt
1 teaspoon ground nutmeg
¼ teaspoon ground ginger
A scant half teaspoon bicarbonate of soda
5 fl.oz. cider

Set oven to 375°F or Mark 5. In a bowl, beat the butter and sugar together until light and fluffy, then add the eggs one at a time, beating well between each addition. Sift together the flour, salt, spices and bicarbonate of soda. Whisk the cider to make it slightly frothy, then fold it into the mixture, alternately with the dry ingredients. Combine well together and turn the mixture into a well-greased and base-lined 7-8 inch square cake tin. Smooth the top and bake for 50-60 minutes or until the cake is golden brown and springy to the touch. Allow to cool in the tin for 5 minutes, then turn out on to a wire rack. Store the cake in an airtight tin for one day before cutting. Though it is not traditional, 2 oz. sultanas that have been soaked in 2 tablespoons of cider overnight, can be added to the mixture.

"The End of the Day" by William Millner

Apple, Raisin and Cider Teabread

A good, fruity, apple flavoured teatime treat.

8 oz. self-raising flour
¼ teaspoon salt
1 level teaspoon mixed spice
4 oz. butter
3 oz. soft brown sugar
1 medium cooking apple, peeled, cored and finely chopped
3 oz. raisins soaked in 2 tablespoons cider
2 medium eggs

GLAZE

2 oz. soft brown sugar
2 tablespoons cider

Set oven to 350°F or Mark 4. Butter a 2 lb loaf tin. Sieve the flour, salt and spice into a bowl and rub in the butter until the mixture resembles fine breadcrumbs. Stir in the sugar, chopped apple and raisin/cider mixture. Add the eggs and mix well. Put the mixture into the loaf tin and bake for approximately one hour until golden and firm and when a skewer inserted comes out clean. Turn out to cool on a wire rack. Boil the glaze ingredients together in a pan for 3 or 4 minutes and brush over the warm loaf. Serve sliced, plain or buttered.

Cider-Baked Pears

This simple recipe is a good way of serving the hard, cooking pears found in many Dorset country gardens.

1 oz. soft brown sugar ½ pint medium dry cider
6 pears, peeled, halved and cored
1 oz. butter
Chopped walnuts for sprinkling

Set oven to 350°F or Mark 4. In a saucepan, dissolve the sugar in the cider over a low heat, bring to the boil and cook for 5 minutes to make a syrup. Arrange the pears in an ovenproof dish and pour the cider syrup over them. Dot with butter, cover and cook in the oven for 30 to 40 minutes until the pears are tender. Cool, sprinkle with walnuts and serve with clotted cream.

“May Day” by Thomas Chambers

Wassail Bowl

This Old English punch is an ideal and warming drink after carol singing at Christmas.

1 quart ale
½ bottle sherry
1 teaspoon freshly grated nutmeg
1 teaspoon ground ginger
1 teaspoon ground cinnamon
2 slices of toast
Juice and rind of 1 lemon
2 medium sized baked apples, chopped
Sugar to taste
1 orange

Mix all the ingredients in a large saucepan. Heat the mixture but *do not* let it boil. Allow to stand for 1 hour. Strain and re-heat. Serve either in a large bowl with slices of orange floating on the surface or in individual mugs or tumblers each with a slice of orange. If using glass tumblers make sure that the mixture is not too hot.

Spicy Stewed Pears

Ripe pears picked off the tree are a real taste of autumn. This adaptation of an old Worcestershire recipe combines another autumn fruit – blackberries – with the pears. Comice pears are ideal for this dish but are not essential.

6 pears	**¼-½ pint sweet cider**
½ lb. blackberries	**1 teaspoon dried mixed spice**
¼-½ pint red wine	**½-1 teaspoon ground ginger**

Wash the blackberries well and peel the pears and leave whole. Put the fruits together into a saucepan, pour on the red wine and add the mixed spice and ground ginger. Gently poach the fruit over a low heat until tender. Remove the pears, cut each one in half, carefully remove the cores and return to the pan. Now just cover with sweet cider, bring to the boil and boil rapidly until the liquid is reduced and syrupy. Serve with whipped cream. Serves 6.

Buttered Apples

This quickly made farmhouse pudding from Herefordshire would usually be served with cider sauce.

1 lb. cooking apples weighed after peeling and coring
6 oz. sugar 6 oz. butter
3 thick slices stale bread, crusts removed and cut into cubes
A little extra sugar (optional)

CIDER SAUCE
1 pint cider ¼ lb. sugar 2 to 3 oz. butter

Cut the apples into slices and roll in the sugar until completely coated. Melt half the butter in a frying pan and fry the apples until golden brown and soft. Keep warm on a serving dish. Melt the remaining butter in the pan and fry the bread cubes until golden brown and crisp. Lightly combine with the apples, sprinkle over a little extra sugar, if desired and serve at once, accompanied by hot Cider Sauce or whipped cream. Serves 4 to 6.

CIDER SAUCE: Simmer the cider and sugar together in a pan, to form a light syrup, stirring from time to time. Cut the butter into small pieces and whisk into the mixture. Pour into a sauce boat and serve at once.

METRIC CONVERSIONS

The weights, measures and oven temperatures used in the preceding recipes can be easily converted to their metric equivalents. The conversions listed below are only approximate, having been rounded up or down as may be appropriate.

Weights

Avoirdupois	Metric
1 oz.	just under 30 grams
4 oz. (¼ lb.)	app. 115 grams
8 oz. (½ lb.)	app. 230 grams
1 lb.	454 grams

Liquid Measures

Imperial	Metric
1 tablespoon (liquid only)	20 millilitres
1 fl. oz.	app. 30 millilitres
1 gill (¼ pt.)	app. 145 millilitres
½ pt.	app. 285 millilitres
1 pt.	app. 570 millilitres
1 qt.	app. 1.140 litres

Oven Temperatures

	°Fahrenheit	Gas Mark	°Celsius
Slow	300	2	150
	325	3	170
Moderate	350	4	180
	375	5	190
	400	6	200
Hot	425	7	220
	450	8	230
	475	9	240

Flour as specified in these recipes refers to plain flour unless otherwise described.